SMOOTHIE DIET

Healthy Smoothie Recipes in a Cookbook for Weight Loss

(Essential Guide Plus Healthy Delicious Ketogenic Diet Smoothie)

Laura Farley

Published by Sharon Lohan

© **Laura Farley**

All Rights Reserved

Smoothie Diet: Healthy Smoothie Recipes in a Cookbook for Weight Loss (Essential Guide Plus Healthy Delicious Ketogenic Diet Smoothie)

ISBN 978-1-990334-45-0

All rights reserved. No part of this guide may be reproduced in any form without permission in writing from the publisher except in the case of brief quotations embodied in critical articles or reviews.

Legal & Disclaimer

The information contained in this book is not designed to replace or take the place of any form of medicine or professional medical advice. The information in this book has been provided for educational and entertainment purposes only.

The information contained in this book has been compiled from sources deemed reliable, and it is accurate to the best of the Author's knowledge; however, the Author cannot guarantee its accuracy and validity and cannot be held liable for any errors or omissions. Changes are periodically made to this book. You must consult your doctor or get professional medical advice before using any of the suggested remedies, techniques, or information in this book.

Table of contents

Part 1 1

Introduction 2

Chapter 1: Green Smoothie Basics 4

Chapter 2: Tips and Tricks for Success 9

Chapter 3: 30 Day Plan Explained 16

Chapter 4: Day 1 25

Breakfast: Fruity, Nutty Pancakes 25

Lunch: Sesame and Ginger Quinoa Salad 27

Dinner: Garlic Chicken with Soy Sauce and Ginger 29

Dessert: Banana Bread with Blueberries 32

Chapter 5: Day 2 34

Breakfast: Huevoes Rancheros with a Spicy Kick 34

Lunch: Kale and Spinach Feta Wrap 37

Dinner: Pasta Topped with Spinach and Homemade Tomato Sauce 39

Dessert: Carrot Cake Muffins 41

Chapter 6: Day 3 43

Breakfast: Tomato Pesto and Eggs Florentine 44

Lunch: Butternut Squash and Lentil Soup 46

Dinner: Tikka Masala 48

Dessert: Fruit and Seed Medley 52

Chapter 7: Day 4 53

Breakfast: Protein Bomb 53

Lunch: Stir Fried shrimp 55

Dinner: Cauliflower and Spicy Noodles 57

Dessert: Cranberry Scones 60

Chapter 8: Day 5 62

Breakfast: Scallions and Corn Muffins 62

Lunch: Kidney Bean Salad with Cucumber, Red Peppers and Corn 65

Dinner: Spicy Quinoa Casserole 67

Dessert: Ginger and Pecan Oatmeal 69

Chapter 9: Day 6 70

Breakfast: Oatmeal with Walnuts 70

Lunch: Avocado and Chicken Salad 72

Dinner: Bean Burger 74

Dessert: Peanut Butter Bars 76

Chapter 10: Day 7 77

Breakfast: Smoked Salmon Frittata with Scallions 78

Lunch: Veggie Burger 80

Dinner: Samosa Stir Fry 82

Dessert: Savory Nut clusters 84

Conclusion 87

Part 2 89

INTRODUCTION 90

BENEFITS OF DRINKING SMOOTHIES 92

200 RECIPES 94

Smoothies for Weight Loss 94

1. Delicious Mango 94

2. Simple Blueberry Smoothie 95

3. Peanut Butter Smoothie 95

4. Blueberry and Yogurt Simple Smoothie 96

5. Decadent Chocolate and Raspberry Smoothie 97

6. Smooth Peaches 97

7. Tangy and Sweet Smoothie 98

8. Simple Apple 99

9. Pineapple Delight 99

10. Strawberry Sweet Smoothie 100

Smoothies that are Kid Friendly 100

11. Strawberry Smoothies with Bananas 101

12. Blazing Blueberry Smoothie 101

13. Elvis Smoothie 102

14. Citrus Smoothie 103

15. Delightful Chocolate Smoothie 103

16. Tropical Extravaganza Smoothie 104

17. Hidden Vegetables Smoothie 104

18. Secret Fiber Smoothie 105

19. The Blue Smoothie 106

20. Peach Attack Smoothie 107

21. Nutella and Strawberry Smoothie 107

Skin Friendly Smoothies 108

22. Smoothie for Clear Skin 108

23. Anti-inflammatory Skin Smoothie 109

24. Skin Boosting Smoothie 110

25. Skin Antioxidants Smoothie 110

26. Tasty Skin Smoothie 111

27. Vitamin C Infusion Smoothie 112

28. Probiotic Smoothie 113

29. Anti-Aging Smoothie 113

30. Healthy Skin Smoothie 114

31. Spicy and Sweet Smoothie 115

High in Fiber Smoothies 116

32. Coffee Smoothie 116

33. Digestive Power Smoothie 117

34. The Green Monster 118

35. Hot Chocolate Smoothie 118

36. Boost Smoothie 119

37. Berry Smoothie with Ginger 120

38. A Mojito to Start Your Day off Right Smoothie................ 121

39. Fig Smoothie.. 121

40. Cinnamon Apple Smoothie 122

41. Kiwi Explosion Smoothie.. 123

Heart Happy Smoothies... 125

42. Green Happiness... 125

43. Up and Ready in the Morning Smoothie 126

44. Chocolate Treat for your Heart....................................... 127

45. Orange Deliciousness 127

46. Green Energy.. 128

47. Red Velvet Smoothie.. 129

48. It Takes Two to Mango Smoothie 130

49. Beat the Blues Smoothie 130

50. Peanut Butter Protein Smoothie.................................... 131

51. Carrot and Papaya Smoothie 132

Muscle Building Smoothies... 133

52. Rise and Shine Smoothie 133

53. Coconut Almond Smoothie... 134

54. Protein Building Monster Smoothie 135

55. Superfood Smoothie 135

56. PB&J Smoothie 136

57. Pomegranate Protein Smoothie 137

58. Strawberry Dream Smoothie 137

59. Sweet Protein and Carrot Smoothie 138

60. Sweet Treat Smoothie 139

61. Pick Me Up Smoothie 139

Exercise Aiding Smoothies 141

62. Banana Bliss 141

63. The K Smoothie 142

64. Cocoa Oat Smoothie 142

65. Blast of Vitamin C Smoothie 143

66. Energy Boosting Smoothie 144

67. Spinach Strength Smoothie 144

68. All Red Smoothie 145

69. The Delicious Green 145

70. Blissful Sweet Smoothie 146

71. Olive Oil Smoothie 147

Detox Smoothies 148

72. Breakfast Smoothie for Winners 148

73. The Original Green Detox Smoothie 149

74. Green Giant Smoothie 149

75. Sweet and Dark Smoothie 150

76. Fiber Packed Smoothie 151

77. Probiotic Filled Smoothie 152

78. Vegetable Delight 152

79. Smooth Operator Smoothie 153

80. Spicy and Nice Smoothie 154

81. Mint Apple Smoothie 154

Immunity Boosting Smoothies 156

82. Orange Pineapple Dream 156

83. Green Tea Smoothie 156

84. Sunrise Smoothie 157

85. Refresh Your Immune System Smoothie 157

86. Ruby Smoothie 158

87. Boost Immunity Smoothie 159

88. Orange Goji Berry Smoothie 160

89. Power Up with Berry and Coconut Smoothie 160

90. Cleanse Out Smoothie 161

91. Go Wild Smoothie 162

Fruit Only Smoothies 163

92. Crazy for Bananas 163

93. Duo Smoothie 163

94. Banana Surprise 164

95. Mango Delight 165

96. Pretty in Pink Smoothie 165

97. Peanut Butter Blueberry Smoothie 166

98. Banana Mango Smoothie 166

99. Watermelon Strawberry Smoothie 167

100. Sparkling Watermelon Smoothie 167

101. Stay Peachy Smoothie 168

Veggie Smoothies 169

102. Cucumber Spa Smoothie 169

103. Super Green Smoothie 169

104. Yam Smoothie 170

105. Zucchini Simplicity Smoothie 171

106. Broccoli Smoothie 171

107. Salad Smoothie 172

108. Rhubarb Smoothie 173

109. Veggie Delicious Smoothie 173

110. Cabbage Smoothie 174

111. Zucchini and Carrot Delight Smoothie 175

112. Spinach Smoothie with a Fruit Blast 175

Simple Smoothies 177

113. Triple Berry Surprise 177

114. Almond Smoothie 178

115. Cantaloupe Smoothie 178

116. The Apple Carrot Smoothie 179

117. Creamy Date Smoothie 179

118. Simply Mango Smoothie 180

119. Apple Kale Smoothie 180

120. Banana Cashew Smoothie 181

121. Nutty Raspberry Smoothie 182

122. Flax Strawberry Smoothie 182

CONCLUSION 183

Part 1

Introduction

When it comes to improving your overall quality of life, there are few better things you can do for your body than purify it of all the unhealthy toxins that build up naturally over the years and making the decision to take charge of your diet and improve yourself is a decision worth celebrating.

Unfortunately deciding to make a positive change in your diet is much easier than actually going through with what needs to be done in order to do so which is why the following chapters will discuss everything you need in order to get started on your new lifestyle and stick with it in the long term. First you will learn all about the many benefits that green smoothies can have when it comes to detoxifying your system and helping you lose weight as quickly and easily as possible. From there, you will then be provided with an outline of a meal plan that will further compound the process and make it easier for you to succeed. Finally, you will be provided with 60 different green smoothie recipes to ensure that you can find the smoothie (or smoothies) that are right for you.

There are plenty of books on this subject on the market, thanks again for choosing this one! Every effort was made to ensure it is full of as much useful information as possible, please enjoy!

Chapter 1: Green Smoothie Basics

When it comes to easily getting all the nutrients that you need for the day while at the same time losing weight and detoxifying your system, there are few better options available than a green smoothie. While the idea of the green smoothie is relatively straight forward, any smoothie that is composed of at least 70 percent leafy, dark greens can be said to be green, the space is vast enough that it can be confusing for those just starting out to know where to begin. While the specifics might vary, all green smoothies are sure to share a variety of health benefits, regardless of the specific fruits and vegetables that you choose to use.

Easily digestible
Studies have proven that vegetables and fruits that have been blended together are naturally healthier than if those same vegetables and fruits were consumed in their natural state. While this might seem counterintuitive, the blending process breaks down the

cell walls present in the cells of all plants, making it easier for your body to extract the required nutrients in the process. In a nutshell, the blending process acts as the initial stages of digestion leaving your body free to expend its energy on absorbing as much nutrition from the things that you put into it as possible. As an added bonus, the fiber found in green smoothies also improves digestion overall by forcing your colon to work overtime.

Brimming with nutrition

With 70 percent of every smoothie being made up of healthy greens, it stands to reason that each smoothie you consume is going to run the gamut when it comes to vitamins and minerals. They are also known to contain a dramatically higher concentration of antioxidants and polyphenols which are extremely important when it comes to fighting off degenerative diseases, including cancer. Pound for pound, when compared to juices made from the same raw materials, smoothies contain nearly five times as much fiber as well.

Great replacement for caffeine

While caffeine is a great way to get an extra burst of energy in a short period of time, it is largely void of any real nutritional value. Compare this with the average green smoothie which is so full of vitamins and nutrients that the energy it provides is enough to give a jolt to the system practically on par with a cup of coffee. This makes green smoothies a great way to start the day or to get you through the midafternoon doldrums in style.

Excellent way to detoxify your system

When it comes to initiating a 30-day detox, green smoothies are a natural choice for flushing your system of a wide variety of toxins. They are so effective thanks to the high amount of chlorophyll that they contain which naturally encourages the cells in the human body to release toxins that they have been holding onto for years, if not decades. The previously mentioned high amounts of fiber also stimulate the colon to ensure it is active for its part of the detoxification process as well.

What's more, it doesn't take a massive amount of green smoothie consumption to begin seeing these benefits either, nor does it require a radical restructuring of your diet beyond simply making a concentrated effort to eat healthy and avoid foods that are naturally high in toxins. For most people two servings of a green smoothie per day is enough to start seeing real results if they keep it up for just a few weeks.

Easy to make and very portable

One of the biggest reasons that many people find themselves unable to maintain a healthy diet is that it can be difficult to find healthy foods on the go. The green smoothie takes care of these concerns as practically all green smoothies can be ready to go in less than 5 minutes and each preparation can easily make 2 or more servings. As long as there is a cool place for storage, most of the smoothies in the following pages will keep for about 24 hours meaning that 5 minutes in the morning is all you need to set yourself up for success for the entire day.

Something for everyone

The 70/30 split for a proper green smoothie means that they are sure to be palatable both for dedicated vegetarians as well as those who believe that vegetables are strictly only what real food eats. Thirty percent fruit is enough to cut the flavors of many of the healthiest vegetable to a point that you won't even know they are there. While it might take you a few days to adapt to the taste, your pallet will typically adapt within as little as 7 days and you will be surprised how quickly you start to crave a healthy alternative to sugary snacks or a quick fast food meal that is completely devoid of all nutritional content.

Chapter 2: Tips and Tricks for Success

Choose the right blender for the job

For those just getting into the smoothie game, the wide variety of potential tools can make it difficult to separate the wheat from the chaff. First and foremost, it is important to look for a powerful blender instead of a juicer. A juicer extracts the essence of fruits and vegetables, leaving all of the healthy pulp and all of its related nutrients behind. Rather, you are going to want to invest in a blender, and a quality one at that, in order to make your green smoothie transition as easy as possible.

When it comes to choosing a blender the first thing that you are going to want to consider is the quality of the motor to ensure that it will be able to stand up to all of the stress of daily blending that you will be subjecting it too. While they are going to be more expensive, it is recommended that you choose a blender that is 1000 watts or more which will ensure that it is able to fully liquify anything that crosses its path. To ensure that it lives up to your standards, you should also make sure it has a warranty that is good for a year, if not longer. Finally, you want to ensure that it has a nice wide mouth and enough room to hold about 40 ounces of liquid if you don't want to have to blend multiple times each day.

If you already have a blender that you feel is mostly adequate to the task at hand, and you don't relish spending approximately $400 on the type of blender that makes smoothie making as easy as possible, there are a number of things you can do to ensure that your smoothies turn out as smooth as possible. First you are going to want to ensure that you always add any liquid ingredients first as this will create more suction in your blender which will pull any other ingredients you add more fully into the blades. Depending on the strength of your blender, as much as 16 ounces of liquid might be required.

Next, if the smoothie that you are making contains fruit, it is important to add it in before you start in on the greens. This only goes for fresh fruit, however, as frozen fruit should only be added after any fresh ingredients but before any extra ice you may be inclined to add. Adding the fruit before the vegetables will help to ensure that there is enough suction to get the vegetables right down next to the blades where they can do the most good.

When it comes to vegetables, you are going to want to pre-chop, shred or dice your ingredients based on the strength of your blender's motor. If you have a standard 300-watt motor you will want to avoid adding anything that has a diameter greater than 1 inch with weaker motors requiring even smaller pieces. This is one of the most compelling to go with either a Blendtec or Vitamix blender as their stronger motors will save you a significant amount of time in the long run.

To reach the right blending consistency, you are going to want to vary the speed on your blender while also making judicious use of the pulse button. Pulsing at the start will like break up many of the more hearty parts of your smoothie and make the rest of the blending process much easier as a result. Once you have started things moving with the pulse button, you will then want to slowly work your way up the speeds at your disposal, increasing the speed approximately every 30 seconds. If you have to stop in the middle of the process for any reason it is recommended that you start off at the slowest speed when you resume and repeat the process.

If your smoothies end up being more of a food that you chew rather than a liquid that you drink, you may find it effective to pulse for up to two minutes prior to starting the alternating speed process. If you still aren't getting the results that you would like you may need to start with any liquids or berries that you are using and blending them completely before adding in your greens in two or more phases, slowly working up to the tougher vegetables. Even with an underpowered blender you should be able to ultimately create an acceptable smoothie, it will just take much longer and be a more elaborate process than something with the power to get it all done at once.

Take it slow

If the smoothies that you end up with are still a little on the chewy side, it is important to pace yourself during consumption to give your body the opportunity to digest all of the plant matter that you are suddenly consuming. While this is not an issue if your smoothie doesn't require any chewing, if you do find yourself masticating more than you would like then the enzymes in your stomach are likely working overtime and overloading them is a great way to give yourself a stomachache.

The same thing can occur with non-organic fruit and vegetables of the sort that are commonly found in traditional grocery stores. While organic fruits and vegetables are recommended as they typically are more nutritious and contain fewer chemicals and pesticides, using more traditional produce is acceptable as long as you scrub each ingredient thoroughly to ensure you are avoiding consuming a large amount of potential dangerous chemicals. The most reliable way to ensure your fruits and vegetables are chemical and pesticide free is to soak them for anywhere from 15 to 20 minutes in a mixture of water combined with .5 cups of apple cider vinegar and then rinsing each off individually.

Add variety to your diet
When you are first starting out with green smoothies, it can be easy to find a few different recipes that you like and stick with them to the exclusion of everything else. While understandable, this mindset deprives you of one of the greatest strengths of the green smoothie, the variety that is inherent in the fruits and vegetables that become available with the changing of the

seasons. Different fruits and vegetables have different levels of many different vitamins and nutrients and following the changing of the seasons is a quick and easy way to ensure that you are getting a well-round and varied diet. What's more, mixing things up gives you an opportunity to find new favorites that you never would have discovered otherwise.

Chapter 3: 30 Day Plan Explained

The following chapters contain 7 days worth of meals, breakfasts, lunches, dinners and desserts, chosen with the aim to help you detox your system as effectively as possible while at the same time helping you to lose weight along the way. In addition to following the suggested meal plan you should plan on drinking one or two of the smoothies listed in chapter 11 to kick your 30-day detox into high gear. Once you have tried the meals in the order in which they are listed, from there you are free to mix and match for the remainder of the 30 days to create a meal plan that is unique for you. Below is the shopping list for the first 7 days.

Vegetables

- Avocado (5)
- Red cabbage (1)
- Chili (1)
- Carrots (15)
- Yellow pepper (1)

- Edamame (1.5 c)
- Spearmint leaves (12)
- Cucumber (1)
- Garlic (16 cloves)
- Broccoli (4 heads)
- Red bell pepper (9)
- Scallions (19)
- Sun dried tomatoes (1 T)
- Spinach (32 oz)
- Kale (1 c)
- Mushrooms (.25 c)
- Basil (1.5 c)
- Pepperoncino peppers (2)
- Tomatoes (5, 2 lb canned)
- Tomato pesto (.25 c)
- Butternut squash (2)
- Celery (3 stalks)
- Yellow Onion (1)
- Vegetable broth (8 c)
- Onion (5)
- Chives (1 bunch)

- Green Beans (1 lb)
- Orange Pepper (1)
- Yellow pepper (1)
- Cauliflower (1 head)
- Corn kernels (3.5 c)
- Cilantro (1 c)
- Cherry Tomatoes (1 c)
- English cucumber (1)
- Green onion (6)
- Baby potatoes (2 lbs)
- Peas (1 cup frozen)
- Black olive tapenade (.75 c)
- Sweet potato (1)
- Sunflower sprouts (1 handful)

Grains

- Quinoa (4.25 c)
- Corn tortilla 6 inch (8)
- Wheat tortilla 7 inch (1)
- Wheat spaghetti (1 lb)
- English muffin (3)

- Whole grain crackers (5)
- Rice noodles (1 lb)
- Steel cut oats (.25 c)
- Rolled oats (1.25 c)
- Rice (1 c)
- Barley (.25 c)
  - Farro (.3 c)

Meat

- Chicken breast (2.5 lb)
- Shrimp (1.5 lbs)
- Smoked Salmon (2 oz)

Beans

- White beans (1 can)
- Red lentils (1 can)
- Kidney beans (1 can)
- Black beans (1 can)
- Garbanzo beans (1 can)
- Baked beans (1 can)

Eggs/Dairy

- Egg (24)
- Buttermilk (1 c)
- Plain Greek Yogurt (5 c)
- Sour cream (.25 c)
- Feta Cheese (2 T)
- Vanilla yogurt fat free (24 oz)
- Pecorino Romano cheese (2 T)
- Milk (4 c)
- Paneer (16 oz)
- Soy milk (2.5 c)
- Cheddar cheese (1 oz)
- Mozzarella cheese (16 oz)
- Lemon yogurt (6 oz)

Seasonings/Sweeteners

- Ketchup (2 T)
- Honey (1.25 c)
- Cinnamon (1.75 tsp ground)
- Vanilla extract (2 tsp)
- Ginger (7 inches)

- Rice vinegar (1 c)
- Red pepper flakes (2 T)
- Arrowroot powder (6.5 tsp)
- Soy sauce (1 c)
- Hot sauce (6 oz)
- Salsa (4 T)
- Chicken bone broth (.5 c)
- Cumin (2.5 tsp)
- Vanilla (1 tsp)
- Black pepper (4 T)
- Lime juice (1 T)
- Lemon juice (1 tsp)
- Nutmeg (.75 tsp)
- Peanut butter (.5 c)
- Cardamom (.5 tsp)
- Cloves (3)
- Paprika (3 T)
- Coriander (.5 c)
- Turmeric (1 T)
- Red chili powder (1 tsp)
- Miso (2 T)

- Gingersnap (1)
- Chocolate chips (.25 c)
- Taco seasoning (1 T)
- Maple syrup (3 T)
- Cayenne pepper (2.25 tsp)
- Garam masala (2 tsp)
- Tarragon (.5 tsp)
- Parsley (2 T)
- Mayonnaise (.25 c)

Fruits

- Raspberries (1.5 c)
- Blueberries (2 c)
- Lemon (1)
- Crushed pineapple (1.5 c)
- Cranberries (1 cups)
- Apple Juice (.5 c)
- Goji Berries (.25 c)

Oils/Butter

- Canola oil (3 c)

- Margarine (3 T)
- Sesame Oil (4 T)
- Olive oil (16 T)
- Extra virgin olive oil (4 T)
- Flaxseed oil (4 T)
- Coconut oil (1 T)

Nuts/Seeds

- Walnuts (1 c chopped)
- Sesame seeds (1 T)
- Chia seeds (.5 oz)
- Flax seeds (.5 oz)
- Pomegranate seeds (.5 oz)
- Fenugreek seeds (1 T)
- Almond milk (.3 c)
- Pecans (1.25 c)
- Cashews (.3 c)
- Almonds (2 c)

Baking

- Celtic salt (10 tsp)

- Sea salt (2 tsp)
- Baking soda (2.5 tsp)
- Baking powder (17 T)
- Sugar (2 c)
- Yellow cornmeal (2 c)
- Whole wheat flour (5.25 c)
- All-purpose flour (4.25 c)
- Pancake mix (1.5 c)
- Brown sugar (4 T)

Chapter 4: Day 1

Breakfast: Fruity, Nutty Pancakes

For this recipe, you will need to set aside 10 minutes for preparation, 20 minutes of cooking time and the results will feed 4.

Nutrition Information

255 calories

10 g of protein

387 mg of sodium

5 g of fiber

2 g of fat (saturated)

67 g of carbs

15 g of fat

Ingredients-Pancake Batter

- Whole wheat flour (1.5 c)
- Sugar (6 T)
- Salt (.5 tsp)
- Baking powder (1 T)

- Flour (1.5 c)
- Baking soda (1 tsp)

Ingredients-Pancakes

- Buttermilk (1 c)
- Egg (1)
- Water (.25 c)
- Cinnamon (.25 tsp)
- Banana (1 thinly sliced)
- Canola oil (1 T)
- Pancake mix (1.3 c)
- Raspberries (.5 c)
- Vanilla extract (1 tsp)
- Honey (.3 c)
- Water (1 T)
- Walnuts (.5 c chopped)

Cooking instructions

- Place the cornmeal, both types of flour, baking powder, sugar, baking soda and salt into a mixing bowl and combine thoroughly.

- Take 1.3 c of the results and mix with the cinnamon in a separate bowl.
- In yet another bowl, combine the buttermilk, egg, water, vanilla extract and canola oil and mix thoroughly before adding in the banana slices.
- In a final bowl, combine the walnuts, honey and 1 T water.
- Prepare a skillet before setting it on the stove above a burner set to medium.
- .25 c of batter will make one pancake. Each side of each pancake will need to cook for approximately 2 minutes.
- Top the finished pancakes using the honey mixture and the raspberries.

Lunch: Sesame and Ginger Quinoa Salad

For this recipe, you will need to set aside 10 minutes for preparation, 15 minutes of cooking time and the results will feed 4.

Nutrition Information

363 calories

15 g of protein

197 mg of sodium

8 g of fiber

2 g of fat (saturated)

43 g of carbs

14 g of fat

Ingredients

- Water (2 c)
- Edamame (1.5 c)
- Quinoa (1 c rinsed)
- Salt (.25 tsp)
- Carrots (3 medium diced)
- Chili (.5 diced)
- Yellow pepper (.5 diced)
- Sesame oil (2 T)
- Rice vinegar (2 T)
- Red cabbage (1 c chopped)
- Sesame seeds (1 T)
- Ginger (.4 tsp)

Cooking instructions

- Turn a boiler to a high heat before combining the water, quinoa and salt together in a covered pot and placing the pot on the boiler. After it reaches the boiling point reduce the heat to low and let the quinoa cook 15 minutes or until the water is completely absorbed.
- Combine the peppers, carrots, cabbage, edamame and the quinoa in a bowl and mix well.
- Separately in another bowl, combine the ginger, sesame oil, rice vinegar and sesame seeds together and mix well.
- Combine the two bowls prior to serving.

Dinner: Garlic Chicken with Soy Sauce and Ginger

For this recipe, you will need to set aside 20 minutes for preparation, 12 minutes of cooking time and the results will feed 4.

Nutrition Information

394 calories

51 g of protein

1120 mg of sodium

2.8 g of fiber

1 g of fat (saturated)

25 g of carbs

10.4 g of fat

Ingredients
- Soy sauce (.5 c)
- Arrowroot powder (3.5 tsp)
- Ginger (2 T chopped)
- Water (.5 c)
- Honey (.25 c)
- Broccoli (16 oz)
- Garlic (2 cloves)
- Chicken breast (2 lbs)
- Olive oil (2 T)
- Carrots (4 sliced)
- Red pepper flakes (as needed)

Cooking instructions

- In a small bowl, mixt together the arrowroot powder, water, honey and soy sauce.
- Place the results into a sauce pan before setting the pan above a burner to a medium/low. Allow the sauce 5 minutes to thicken, stir approximately once per minute.
- Set a large skillet above a burner turned to medium/high and coat it with the olive oil. Add in the chicken as well as the carrots stirring regularly and let it cook approximately 7 minutes before adding in the garlic and cooking another minute.
- While waiting for the chicken to cook, microwave the broccoli until it is cooked to your desired level of firmness.
- Once the broccoli has cooked, add the sauce to the skillet and mix well.
- Top with red pepper flakes as desired before serving.

Dessert: Banana Bread with Blueberries

For this recipe, you will need to set aside 10 minutes for preparation, 40 minutes of cooking time and the results will feed 16.

Nutrition Information

197 calories

5 g of protein

134 mg of sodium

2 g of fiber

1 g of fat (saturated)

29 g of carbs

8 g of fat

Ingredients
- Baking soda (.5 tsp)
- Banana (3)
- Avocado (.25 c)
- Sugar (.75 c)
- Baking soda (.5 tsp)
- Salt (1 tsp)

- Whole wheat flour (.5 c)
- Baking powder (1 tsp)
- Whole wheat flour (.5 c)
- Vanilla extract (1 tsp)
- Eggs (3)
- Blueberries (.5 c)
- Water (3 T)
- Margarine (3 T)

Cooking instructions
- Set your oven to 350 degrees F beforehand
- Combine the baking soda and the bananas in a mixing bowl.
- In another bowl, combine the avocado, sugar and margarine before then adding in the eggs one by one. Next, add in the salt, baking powder, all of the flour and mix enough for the ingredients to begin to combine.
- Combine the two bowls before adding in the water and vanilla, finally fold in the blueberries.

- Add the results to two 8 in loaf pans and let them bake for 40 minutes. The bread is finished when an inserted toothpick comes out clean.
- Cool 5 minutes prior to serving.

Chapter 5: Day 2

Breakfast: Huevoes Rancheros with a Spicy Kick

For this recipe, you will need to set aside 10 minutes for preparation, 16 minutes of cooking time and the results will feed 4.

Nutrition Information

331 calories

16 g of protein

245 mg of sodium

10 g of fiber

3 g of fat (saturated)

42 g of carbs

12 g of fat

Ingredients

- White beans (16 oz)
- Red bell pepper (1 stripped)
- Cumin (1 tsp)
- Scallions (4 sliced)
- Garlic (2 minced cloves)
- Chicken broth (.5 c)
- Plain Greek Yoghurt (4 T)
- Avocado (1 c peeled, sliced)
- Eggs (4)
- Hot sauce (as needed)
- Salsa (4 T)
- Six-inch corn tortillas (8)

Cooking instructions

- Apply cooking spray to your skillet before placing it on the stove above a burner set to a medium/high heat.

- Add the cumin to the skillet and allow it 30 seconds to cook, stirring continuously. Once it becomes fragrant, mix in the red bell pepper, chicken broth, scallions, garlic and beans.
- Allow the ingredients in the skillet to boil before turning the heat down and letting everything simmer for 8 minutes until the skillet is nearly devoid of broth. Once this occurs mash the beans until the results are lumpy.
- Create 4 separate indentations in the beans before cracking the eggs and adding one to each indentation.
- Place a lid on your skillet and let the eggs cook until they reach the state which you prefer.
- Split the results in the skillet into 4 before topping with the avocado, salsa, yoghurt and hot sauce. Serve with tortillas.

Lunch: Kale and Spinach Feta Wrap

For this recipe, you will need to set aside 10 minutes for preparation, 6 minutes of cooking time and the results will feed 1.

Nutrition Information

252 calories

16.2 g of protein

600 mg of sodium

5 g of fiber

4.5 g of fat (saturated)

23 g of carbs

11 g of fat

Ingredients

- Mushrooms (.25 c sliced)
- Spinach (1 c)
- Feta cheese (2 T)
- Whole wheat tortilla (7 in)
- Black pepper (.25 tsp)
- Kale (1 c)

- Sun dried tomatoes (1 T chopped)
- Egg (1)
- Egg white (1 whisked)

Cooking instructions

- Warm the tortilla by placing it in the microwave and letting it cook for 1 minute on the standard power setting.
- At the same time, coat a skillet using cooking spray before placing it on the stop above a burner turned to a medium heat. Place the mushrooms into the skillet before seasoning with the pepper and letting them cook for 2 minutes.
- Mix in the spinach and let it cook until it begins to wilt which should take approximately another 2 minutes.
- Mix in the egg and let them cook until they have begun to set which should take approximately 2 more minutes.

- Place the results into the tortilla and top with the feta cheese and chopped sun dried tomato prior to serving.

Dinner: Pasta Topped with Spinach and Homemade Tomato Sauce

For this recipe, you will need to set aside 25 minutes for preparation, 12 minutes of cooking time and the results will feed 4.

Nutrition Information

399 calories

14.5 g of protein

818 mg of sodium

9 g of fiber

4 g of fat (saturated)

41 g of carbs

15.5 g of fat

Ingredients

- Whole wheat spaghetti (1 lb)

- Garlic (4 cloves chopped)
- Fresh spinach (10 oz)
- Pecorino Romano cheese (2 T)
- Tomatoes (4 chopped)
- Dried pepperoncino peppers (2 chopped)
- Sea salt (1 tsp)
- Basil (.5 c chopped)
- Extra virgin olive oil (2.5 T)

<u>Cooking instructions</u>
- Place the pasta into a medium-sized pot and let it cook according to the provided directions
- While the pasta is cooking, place your skillet onto the stove above a burner turned to a medium heat. Coat the skillet using the olive oil before adding in the pepperoncino peppers and letting them cook for 60 seconds before mixing in the garlic and letting the results cook until the garlic begins to smell fragrant but has not yet burned.
- Mix in the tomatoes and let them cook for 10 minutes or until they are fully cooked and a little

soft, stir regularly. Top with the cheese and add in the salt before pouring the results into an immersion blender to thoroughly combine the ingredients.
- Add the results back into the skillet and then add in the basil, spinach and pasta.
- Combine well prior to serving.

Dessert: Carrot Cake Muffins

For this recipe, you will need to set aside 10 minutes for preparation, 25 minutes of cooking time and the results will feed 12.

Nutrition Information

209 calories

9 g of protein

226 mg of sodium

1 g of fiber

2 g of fat (saturated)

32 g of carbs

6 g of fat

Ingredients

- Flour (1.25 c)
- Salt (.25 tsp)
- Whole wheat flour (.5 c)
- Cinnamon (1 tsp)
- Baking soda (.25 tsp)
- Baking powder (1 tsp)
- Sour cream (.25 c)
- Cream cheese (.5 c)
- Canola oil (2 T)
- Sugar (2.5 T)
- Vanilla (1 tsp)
- Brown sugar (2.5 T)
- Egg (1)
- Carrots (1 c)
- Pineapple (.5 c crushed)

Cooking instructions

- Set your oven ahead of time to 375 degrees F
- Place muffin cups into a 12-slot muffin tin

- In a small mixing bowl combine the sugar, cream cheese and egg together and mix well before adding in the pineapple as well as the carrots
- In a separate bowl, mix together the sour cream, canola oil, sugar and brown sugar and blend well before mixing in the vanilla.
- Ensure there is space in the dry ingredients for the wet ingredients before coming the two bowls and mixing well. Take care not to overmix.
- Fill the muffin tins with the results, taking care to leave room in each space for the baked muffin to rise.
- Add the tin to the preheated oven and bake for 20 minutes. The muffins will be fully cooked when you can stick a toothpick into the center of the center muffins and it comes out clean.
- Allow the muffins 20 minutes to cool before serving.

Chapter 6: Day 3

Breakfast: Tomato Pesto and Eggs Florentine

For this recipe, you will need to set aside 25 minutes for preparation, 5 minutes of cooking time and the results will feed 4.

Nutrition Information

175 calories

12 g of protein

462 mg of sodium

5 g of fiber

2 g of fat (saturated)

21 g of carbs

6 g of fat

Ingredients
- Spinach (10 oz)
- Plain Greek yoghurt (.5 c)
- Olive oil (1 tsp)
- Vinegar (1 tsp)
- Sun dried tomato pesto (.25 cups)

- Eggs (4 large)
- Black pepper (as needed)
- Salt (1 pinch)
- English muffin (2 toasted)

Cooking instructions

- Use the olive oil to prepare the skillet before adding it to the stove above a burner set to a medium/high heat.
- Add in the spinach and let it cook for approximately 2 minutes until it begins to wilt. Once this happens, add in the tomato pesto along with the Greek yoghurt and mix well. Remove the skillet from the stove.
- Pour 1 in of water into a saucepan before placing the pan on the stove above a burner that is set to a high heat. Let the water boil and then add in the vinegar along with the salt before turning the heat to low.
- Place one of the eggs into a cup and then add it gently to the water, repeating the process with the

remaining eggs. Place a lid on the skillet and allow the eggs to simmer for about 5 minutes, shaking the pan once every 1.5 minutes.

- Split the English muffins in two before placing each on a plate before toping it with some of the spinach. Use a slotted spoon to top each muffin with an egg.
- Add what is left into the skillet before combining it with the pesto and yogurt and mix thoroughly prior to topping each muffin with the results.

Lunch: Butternut Squash and Lentil Soup

For this recipe, you will need to set aside 5 minutes for preparation, 8 hours of cooking time and the results will feed 8.

Nutrition Information

253 calories

18.3 g of protein

792 mg of sodium

17 g of fiber

0 g of fat (saturated)

41 g of carbs

2 g of fat

Ingredients
- Vegetable broth (8 c)
- Red lentils (2 c)
- Nutmeg (.5 tsp)
- Yellow onion (1 chopped)
- Carrots (3 sliced)
- Butternut squash (3 c diced)
- Garlic (2 cloves minced)

Cooking instructions
- In a slow cooker, add the yellow onion, butternut squash, vegetable broth, red lentils, carrots, garlic and celery.
- Place a lid on the slow cooker before turning it to a low heat and letting it cook for 8 hours. You can also cook the soup for 5 hours if you use a high heat instead.

- The resulting soup can be successfully stored in the refrigerator for approximately 3 days, after that it should be moved to the freezer.

Dinner: Tikka Masala

For this recipe, you will need to set aside 45 minutes for preparation, 20 minutes of cooking time and the results will feed 6.

Nutrition Information

525 calories

19 g of protein

700 mg of sodium

0 g of fiber

1.5 g of fat (saturated)

28 g of carbs

15 g of fat

Ingredients-Gravy

- Sea salt (1 tsp)
- Canned tomatoes (1 lb, chopped)

- Olive oil (3 T)
- Ginger (2 in)
- Water (2 c)
- Carrots (2 chopped)
- Garlic (4 cloves, chopped)
- Red bell pepper (1 chopped)
- Onion (4 chopped)

Ingredients-Masala

- Nutmeg (.25 tsp)
- Paprika (1 T)
- Cardamom (.5 tsp)
- Cloves (3)
- Cinnamon (.5 tsp)
- Cumin (1 T)
- Coriander (1 T)
- Fenugreek seeds (1 T)
- Turmeric (1 T)
-

Ingredients-Masala

- Red bell peppers (2 chunks)

- Curry gravy (3 c)
- Paneer (16 oz)
- Almond milk (.5 c)
- Red chili powder (1 tsp)
- Plain Greek Yoghurt (.3 c)
- Sea salt (1 tsp)
- Coriander (.3 c chopped)
- Milk (.25 cups)
- Arrowroot powder (.5 tsp)

Cooking instructions

- Add the ingredients for the masala mixture, along with the olive oil to a Dutch oven that is a minimum of 6 quarts and then provide the oven with a medium/low heat.
- Cook the spices for 2 minutes which should be enough for them to start to become fragrant. Add in the garlic along with the ginger and let everything cook for approximately 30 seconds and then add in the onions, red bell pepper and carrots and cook everything for an additional 3 minutes.

- Once all the vegetables have cooked, add in the chopped tomatoes along with the water and let the mixture come to a boil. Once this occurs, turn the heat to low and let it simmer for 30 minutes.
- Add the results to an emersion blender and blend until it takes on the consistency of sauce.
- Separately, combine the red chili powder, sea salt, milk, arrowroot powder and plain Greek yoghurt together in a mixing bowl and, after combining thoroughly, add in 3 cups of curry gravy and mix well.
- Place the results into a pan before adding in the paneer along with the red pepper. All the contents of the pan to boil before turning the heat to medium/low and letting everything cook for 15 minutes.
- Turn off the heat before adding in the coriander prior to serving.

Dessert: Fruit and Seed Medley

For this recipe, you will need to set aside 5 minutes for preparation, 0 minutes of cooking time and the results will feed 1.

Nutrition Information

228 calories

5 g of protein

10 mg of sodium

1 g of fiber

3 g of fat (saturated)

25 g of carbs

13 g of fat

Ingredients

- Pomegranate seeds (.5 oz)
- Flax seeds (.5 oz)
- Dried blueberries (2 T)
- Chia seeds (.5 oz)

Cooking instructions

- Add the chia seeds, dried blueberries, pomegranate seeds and flax seeds together in a small bag and shake well.
- Shake again prior to eating and enjoy.

Chapter 7: Day 4

Breakfast: Protein Bomb

For this recipe, you will need to set aside 12 minutes for preparation, 0 minutes of cooking time and the results will feed 1.

Nutrition Information

206 calories

9 g of protein

237 mg of sodium

1 g of fiber

0 g of fat (saturated)

338 g of carbs

2 g of fat

Ingredients
- Reduced fat cheddar cheese (1 oz)
- Whole grain crackers (5)
- Egg (1)

Cooking instructions
- Place the egg into a small pot before adding in enough cold water to ensure that it is completely submerged in 1 in of cold water.
- Place the pot onto the stove over a burner set to a medium/high heat and allow the water in the pot to come to a boil.
- Once the water has boiled, remove the pot from the stove and allow 10 minutes for it to cool completely before draining the pot.
- Add cold water to a small bowl and dunk the egg in it prior to peeling for an easier time of it.

- Remove the shell from the egg and slice it into 5 bite sized sections. Place each section onto a cracker and top with cheese prior to serving.

Lunch: Stir Fried shrimp

For this recipe, you will need to set aside 30 minutes for preparation, 25 minutes of cooking time and the results will feed 4.

Nutrition Information

292 calories

42.9 g of protein

752 mg of sodium

5 g of fiber

2 g of fat (saturated)

17.5 g of carbs

5.5 g of fat

Ingredients
- Deveined shrimp (1.5 lb peeled)
- Green beans (1 lb)

- Miso (2 T)
- Ginger root (3 in peeled, minced)
- Broccoli (1 head florets)
- Rice wine vinegar (.25 c)
- Chives (1 bunch minced)
- Sesame oil (2 T)

Cooking instructions

- Fill a large pot half full of water and place it on top of the stove over a burner set to a high heat. Allow the water to boil and then add in the green beans along with the broccoli before covering and letting the pot simmer on a low heat for 10 minutes.
- While the pot is simmering, use the sesame oil to coat your skillet and then add in the vinegar, miso, chives and ginger root and placing the skill on top of the stove over a burner set to a medium/low heat.
- Let the ingredients in the skillet cook for 10 minutes prior to adding in the shrimp. Let the shrimp cook for 5 minutes. Once the shrimp begin to curl and

turn opaque flip them and cook for another 5 minutes.
- Combine all of the ingredients prior to serving.

Dinner: Cauliflower and Spicy Noodles

For this recipe, you will need to set aside 20 minutes for preparation, 13 minutes of cooking time and the results will feed 4.

Nutrition Information

324 calories

6 g of protein

1037 mg of sodium

4 g of fiber

2 g of fat (saturated)

48 g of carbs

15 g of fat

Ingredients-Sauce

- Rice wine vinegar (2 T)
- Soy sauce (4 T)

- Unrefined sugar (2 T)
- Ketchup (2 T)
- Arrowroot powder (3 tsp)
- Water (.25 cups)

Ingredients-Meal

- Raw cashews (.3 c)
- Garlic (2 cloves minced)
- Yellow pepper (1 diced)
- Rice noodles (1 lb)
- Red pepper flakes (1 tsp)
- Olive oil (2 T)
- Orange pepper (1 diced)
- Scallion (5)
- Cauliflower (1 head, florets)

Cooking instructions

- Prepare the noodles as per the instructions on the packaging.

- Using a small bowl, combine the unrefined sugar, .25 cups water, ketchup, arrowroot powder, rice wine vinegar and soy sauce together and mix well.
- Spread the olive oil onto your skillet before place it on the stove on top of a burner set to a medium heat. Add in the cauliflower and let it cook 5 minutes, stirring regularly. Remove the cauliflower from the skillet.
- Place the yellow pepper, red pepper and orange pepper into the skillet and allow them to cook for about 3 minutes before placing the cauliflower back into the skillet and letting everything cook for 5 minutes.
- Add in the ginger, garlic and cashews before letting everything cook for 2 minutes and then adding in the sauce.
- Increase the heat beneath the skillet to high and allow the sauce to thicken for 60 seconds.
- Combine the spring onions with the noodles and top with the sauce prior to serving.

Dessert: Cranberry Scones

For this recipe, you will need to set aside 20 minutes for preparation, 20 minutes of cooking time and the results will feed 8.

Nutrition Information

308 calories

6 g of protein

350 mg of sodium

5 g of fiber

1.5 g of fat (saturated)

38 g of carbs

15 g of fat

Ingredients

- Pecans (1 c chopped)
- Salt (.5 tsp)
- Orange zest (1 tsp grated)
- Canola oil (2 T)
- Unsweetened cranberries (.5 c)
- Baking powder (2 tsp)

- Low fat vanilla yogurt (1.25 cups)
- Baking soda (.5 tsp)
- Whole wheat pastry flour (2 c)

Cooking instructions
- Prepare your oven by heating it to 400 degrees F
- Take a 9 in baking pan and coat it with a cooking spray
- Combine the baking soda, salt, baking powder, whole wheat pastry flour and the pecans in a mixing bowl and mix thoroughly.
- Separately, place the vanilla yogurt, orange zest and oil together and whisk briskly.
- Form a place for the wet ingredients in the bowl of dry ingredients and combine the two bowls before adding in the cranberries and blending just enough for all the ingredients to begin to come together.
- Add the contents of the bowl to the 9 in baking pan and then form 8 triangles from the dough using a sharp knife.

- Place the pan in the oven and let the dough bake for 20 minutes. The scones are ready once you can stick a toothpick through the middle of the middle scone and withdraw it cleanly.
- Allow the scones to cool for 5 minutes before eating.

Chapter 8: Day 5

Breakfast: Scallions and Corn Muffins

For this recipe, you will need to set aside 30 minutes for preparation, 25 minutes of cooking time and the results will feed 4.

Nutrition Information

345 calories

9 g of protein

491 mg of sodium

4 g of fiber

1.5 g of fat (saturated)

47 g of carbs

16 g of fat

Ingredients

- Egg (1)
- Brown sugar (2 tsp)
- Egg whites (2)
- Corn kernels (.75 c)
- Salt (.5 tsp)
- Black pepper (to taste)
- Sea salt (1 pinch)
- Fat free plain Greek Yoghurt (1 c)
- Whole wheat pastry flour (.5 c)
- Red bell pepper (1 chopped)
- Yellow cornmeal (1.5 cups)
- Canola oil (2.5 c +2 T divided)
- Scallions (4 thinly sliced)

Cooking instructions

- Prepare your oven by heating it to 350 degrees F and prepare a muffin tin with muffin cups.
- Add the 2 T of canola oil to a skillet before setting it on top of the stove above a burner set to a medium heat.
- Add the bell pepper to the skillet and allow it to cook for 5 minutes. Add the scallions to the skillet and allow them to cook for 1 minute stirring as needed. Remove the skillet from the stove and allow the contents to cool for 5 minutes.
- While the scallions and bell pepper cook, mix together the flour, baking soda, baking powder, black pepper and cornmeal in a mixing bowl.
- Separately, add the remainder of the canola oil along with the egg, egg whites, yoghurt and sugar to another mixing bowl and whisk well. Add in the corn and the bell pepper before combining the two bowls and folding in the dry ingredients until they begin to get moist.
- Add the resulting concoction to the muffin tin and then place the tin in the oven to allow it to bake for

25 minutes. You will know when the muffins are done when you can stick a toothpick into the middle of the middle muffin and pull it out cleanly.
- Allow the muffins to cool for 5 minutes prior to serving.

Lunch: Kidney Bean Salad with Cucumber, Red Peppers and Corn

For this recipe, you will need to set aside 15 minutes for preparation, 0 minutes of cooking time and the results will feed 4.

Nutrition Information

274 calories

10 g of protein

24 mg of sodium

12 g of fiber

2.3 g of fat (saturated)

38 g of carbs

15 g of fat

Ingredients
- Lime (1)
- Corn (1.25 c)
- Red pepper (1 diced)
- Kidney beans (1 can)
- Salt (as needed)
- Black pepper (as needed)
- English cucumber (1 diced)
- Cilantro (.5 c)
- Avocado (1 peeled, diced)
- Cherry tomatoes (1 c)

Cooking instructions
- Using a salad bowl, combine the kidney beans, cherry tomatoes, cilantro, cucumber, red pepper and corn before adding the lime juice and mixing well.
- Mix in the avocado and season as desired with pepper and salt prior to serving.

Dinner: Spicy Quinoa Casserole

For this recipe, you will need to set aside 20 minutes for preparation, 90 minutes of cooking time and the results will feed 8.

Nutrition Information

601 calories

37.5 g of protein

797 mg of sodium

14 g of fiber

6.5 g of fat (saturated)

82 g of carbs

15 g of fat

Ingredients
- Taco seasoning (1 T)
- Sea salt (1.5 tsp)
- Cilantro (.25 c)
- Mozzarella cheese (16 oz)
- Tomatoes (1 lb chopped)
- Hot water (4 c)

- Green onions (6 chopped)
- Corn kernels (8 oz)
- Black beans (15 oz)
- Quinoa (3 c)

Cooking instructions

- Prepare your oven by heating it to 3350 degrees F.
- Using a 9x13 rectangular baking dish add in the sea sat, cilantro, taco season, tomatoes, green onions, quinoa, hot water, corn kernels and mozzarella cheese.
- Use aluminum foil to cover the dish and place it into the oven to cook for 60 minutes.
- Remove the dish from the oven, uncover it, add the rest of the cheese and place it back in the oven to bake for 30 additional minutes.
- Prepare your broiler and place the pan near it to broil for 2 minutes to allow the top of the casserole to brown.
- Serve hot and enjoy

Dessert: Ginger and Pecan Oatmeal

For this recipe, you will need to set aside 10 minutes for preparation, 5 minutes of cooking time and the results will feed 1.

Nutrition Information

200 calories

6 g of protein

15 mg of sodium

3 g of fiber

2 g of fat (saturated)

30 g of carbs

12 g of fat

Ingredients
- Apple juice (.5 c)
- Steel cut oats (.25 c)
- Grapefruit (.5)
- Pecans (1 T chopped)
- Ginger snap (1 crumbled)

Cooking instructions

- Combine the apple juice along with the water in a small saucepan and set it onto the stove over a burner turned to a high heat and allow it to boil.
- Add the oats to the saucepan before reducing the heat to low and allowing the contents of the pan to simmer for 5 minutes, stirring constantly.
- Allow the oatmeal to sit for 2 minutes prior to topping with the gingersnap and pecans and serving.

Chapter 9: Day 6

Breakfast: Oatmeal with Walnuts

For this recipe, you will need to set aside 10 minutes for preparation, 5 minutes of cooking time and the results will feed 4.

Nutrition Information

353 calories

11 g of protein

70 mg of sodium

6 g of fiber

1.5 g of fat (saturated)

57 g of carbs

12 g of fat

Ingredients

- Rolled oats (1.25 c)
- Walnuts (.5 c chopped)
- Unsweetened dried cranberries (.25 c)
- Milk (2.5 c divided)
- Salt (1 tsp)
- Dried goji berries (.25 c)
- Brown sugar (2 tsp)
- Water (1 c)
- Granny smith apple (1 cored)
- Pear (1 quartered)

Cooking instructions

- Combine 1.5 cups of the milk and the water in a saucepan before adding the saucepan to the stove above a burner that has been turned to a high heat.
- Let the water boil before adding in the oats along with the salt and reducing the heat to medium/low to allow the oats to simmer for 3 minutes. Stir regularly to encourage the oats to soften.
- Add in the pear along with the apple before covering the pan and letting everything simmer for three minutes until the fruit tenderizes. Add in the cranberries along with the goji berries before taking the pan off of the burner and letting it sit, covered, for 60 seconds.
- Split the oatmeal into 4 bowls and cover each with 2 T walnuts, .25 cups milk and .5 tsp sugar.
- Serve hot and enjoy.

Lunch: Avocado and Chicken Salad

For this recipe, you will need to set aside 5 minutes for preparation, 0 minutes of cooking time and the results will feed 1.

Nutrition Information

425 calories

39.6 g of protein

405 mg of sodium

8.5 g of fiber

1 g of fat (saturated)

34 g of carbs

15 g of fat

Ingredients
- Shredded chicken (.75 cups cooked)
- Plain Greek yoghurt (2 T)
- English muffin (1)
- Avocado (.25 peeled, sliced)
- Lemon juice (1 tsp)
- Sunflower sprouts (1 handful)
- Tomato (.25 sliced)

Cooking instructions

- Place the avocado is a small bowl and mash it to form a paste before mixing in the plain Greek yoghurt and the lemon juice.
- Add in the chicken and mix well in order to coat it completely
- Plate the English muffin before topping with the sprouts and the chicken prior to serving.

Dinner: Bean Burger

For this recipe, you will need to set aside 30 minutes for preparation, 30 minutes of cooking time and the results will feed 8.

Nutrition Information

165 calories

4 g of protein

462 mg of sodium

3 g of fiber

1.5 g of fat (saturated)

16.5 g of carbs

10.4 g of fat

Ingredients

- Corn kernels (.5 c)
- Salt (.5 tsp)
- Tomato paste (1 T)
- Paprika (2 tsp)
- Mayonnaise (.25 c)
- Olive oil (4 T)
- Egg (1)
- Basil (1 oz)
- Mayonnaise (.25 c)
- Broth (1 c)
- Baked beans (14 oz)
- Organic farro (.3 c)

Cooking instructions

- Soak the farro overnight to ensure it is easy to cook, drain the water from it prior to cooking.
- Place the broth and the faro into a pot and then place the pot on top of a burner set to a high heat.

Once the broth boils, turn the heat to medium/low and let the farro cook for 30 minutes.
- Let the farrow cool before adding all of the ingredients to a mixing bowl and mixing well.
- Form patties from .3 cups of the mixture.
- Add the oil to a skillet before placing the skillet onto a burner turned to a medium heat. Cook the patties for 3 minutes per side.

Dessert: Peanut Butter Bars

For this recipe, you will need to set aside 30 minutes for preparation, 45 seconds of cooking time and the results will feed 6.

Nutrition Information

168 calories

12 g of protein

327 mg of sodium

2 g of fiber

3 g of fat (saturated)

30 g of carbs

16 g of fat

Ingredients

- Cooked rice (1 c)
- Peanut butter (.25 c)
- Maple syrup (2 T)

Cooking instructions

- Add the peanut butter to a bowl that can be microwaved before microwaving it for 45 seconds.
- Combine the maple syrup, rice and peanut butter in a small mixing bowl and mix well.
- Place the peanut butter mixture into an 8x8 glass container and then place the container in the refrigerator to harden for 30 minutes.
- Cut the bars and consume quickly when removed from the refrigerator to prevent the bars from melting.

Chapter 10: Day 7

Breakfast: Smoked Salmon Frittata with Scallions

For this recipe, you will need to set aside 10 minutes for preparation, 15 minutes of cooking time and the results will feed 6.

Nutrition Information

366 calories

10 g of protein

5335 mg of sodium

0 g of fiber

2.5 g of fat (saturated)

1 g of carbs

15 g of fat

Ingredients
- Tarragon (.5 tsp dried)
- Smoked salmon (2 Oz)
- Eggs (4)
- Black olive tapenade (.5 c)
- Scallions (6 chopped)

- Water (.25 c)
- Salt (.5 tsp)
- Egg whites (6)
- Extra virgin olive oil (2 tsp)

Cooking instructions

- Prepare your oven by heating it to 350 degrees F.
- Place the olive oil in a skillet and place the skillet on top of a burner turned to a medium heat. Let the oil heat for 25 seconds and then add in the scallions before letting them cook for 2 minutes, stirring regularly.
- In a small bowl, mix together the eggs, egg whites, water, tarragon and salt and whisk well before seasoning with black pepper.
- Add the contents of the bowl to the skillet and then add in the salmon. Cook all of the ingredients for an addition 2 minutes making sure to stir regularly.
- Add the skillet to the oven and bake for 12 minutes
- Place the tapenade on top before serving.

Lunch: Veggie Burger

For this recipe, you will need to set aside 30 minutes for preparation, 15 minutes of cooking time and the results will feed 6.

Nutrition Information

202 calories

7 g of protein

222 mg of sodium

6 g of fiber

1 g of fat (saturated)

30 g of carbs

6 g of fat

Ingredients

- Parsley (2 T)
- Quinoa (.25 c)
- Barley (.25 c)
- Sweet potato (1)
- Cayenne pepper (1 tsp)
- Garbanzo beans (15 oz)

- Black pepper (.5 tsp)
- Cumin (1.5 tsp)
- Salt (.5 tsp)
- Red peppers (1.5)
- Whole wheat flour (2 T)
- Olive oil (2 T)

Cooking instructions

- Prepare your oven by heating it to 400 degrees F
- Place the sweet potato on a baking tray and place the tray in the oven to bake for 45 minutes until it is nice and soft.
- While the sweet potato is baking, place the quinoa and the barely into two different pots filled with boiling water and let both cook for approximately 40 minutes.
- While the potato is roasting, prepare the red peppers and quarter them before placing them in the oven to roast for 15 minutes.
- Remove the sweet potato from the oven and let it cool before adding it, along with the parsley,

cayenne pepper, flour, black pepper, cumin, salt and 1 T oil into a food processor and process well.
- Place the results in a mixing bowl before adding in the barley and quinoa after they have cooled.
- Place the remaining oil into a skillet before placing the skillet onto the stove above a burner set to a medium heat.
- Place spoonfuls of the bean mix into the skillet and flatten them into patties. Each side of the patty will require approximately 2 minutes to brown properly.
- Place each patty onto a whole-wheat bun and top with roasted peppers before serving.

Dinner: Samosa Stir Fry

For this recipe, you will need to set aside 10 minutes for preparation, 15 minutes of cooking time and the results will feed 4.

Nutrition Information
308 calories
8.4 g of protein

536 mg of sodium

9 g of fiber

1.1 g of fat (saturated)

39 g of carbs

7.5 g of fat

Ingredients

- Sea salt (1 tsp)
- Onion (1 chopped)
- Ginger (2 T chopped)
- Cilantro (.25 cups chopped)
- Baby potatoes (2 lb)
- Peas (1 cup)
- Coriander (2 tsp)
- Olive oil (2 T)
- Garam masala (2 tsp)

Cooking instructions

- Fill a pot 50 percent of the way full of water before placing it on top of a burner turned to a high heat. After the water boils, add in the potatoes and add extra water if they are not submerged by about an inch of water all the way around. Let them cook on the burner for 10 minutes.

- While the potatoes cook, add the olive oil to a skillet before adding in the ginger along with the onion. After the potatoes finish cooking add them in as well.
- Place the skillet on top of a burner turned to a high/medium heat and all the contents of the skillet to cook for 3 minutes, stirring twice a minute. Mix in the spice, peas and salt before cooking an additional 60 seconds.
- Remove the skillet from the stove, mix in the cilantro and serve.

Dessert: Savory Nut clusters

For this recipe, you will need to set aside 10 minutes for preparation, 10 minutes of cooking time and the results will feed 4.

Nutrition Information

200 calories

6 g of protein

287 mg of sodium

4.5 g of fiber

2 g of fat (saturated)

32 g of carbs

12 g of fat

Ingredients
- Salt (.5 tsp)
- Honey (2.5 T)
- Coconut oil (1 T)
- Raw almonds (2 c)
- Maple syrup (1 T)
- Cayenne pepper (.25 tsp)
- Red pepper flakes (1 tsp)

Cooking instructions
- Prepare your oven by heating it to 350 degrees F
- Using a mixing bowl, combine the honey, maple syrup, almonds, coconut oil, cayenne pepper, salt

and red pepper flakes and mix thoroughly to ensure the almonds are well coated.
- Add the almonds to a baking sheet that you have lined with parchment paper before placing the sheet into the oven for 10 minutes. Stir the almonds after 5 minutes to ensure they are well baked.
- Let the almonds cool for 20 minutes to give the glaze time to set prior to serving.

Conclusion

let's hope it was informative and able to provide you with all of the tools you need to achieve your goals whatever it is that they may be. Just because you've finished this book doesn't mean there is nothing left to learn on the topic, expanding your horizons is the only way to find the mastery you seek.

One of the most important things to keep in mind while moving forward is that if you slip and eat something outside the scope of the 30-day plan it isn't the end of the world. Neither should you beat yourself up over your indiscretion unless you use your one mistake as an excuse to go completely off book for several meals or more. Instead, it is much more beneficial to remind yourself of all of the good work that you have done already and to get back on track as quickly as possible. Remember, detoxing and losing weight in a healthy and effective way is a marathon, not a sprint, slow and steady wins the race.

Furthermore, you are going to want to keep in mind that while you are likely to experience an increase in weight loss as your body adjusts to your new diet, it is only natural that this process will curtail itself as time goes on. Losing 1 pound of body fat per week is the average and more than that for too long of time isn't just unrealistic, it is unhealthy no matter what diet you are following. Focus on the physical and mental benefits that are sure to appear as you detoxify your system and let the weight loss take care of itself.

Part 2

INTRODUCTION

Do you deal with weight issues? Do you find that at the end of the day you simply do not have the energy to get everything done? Do you wish to increase immunity in your body? These are all goals of several people throughout the world who feel as though their lives are not whether they had envisioned as a young child. They could be dealing with an inability to lose weight, having more stress, or the like. However, there are methods out there that can help you with weight loss, but also with overall feeling better at the end of the day.

Smoothies have become a huge health trend in the market, as they are helping many people to reclaim their life back. They are easy to make, and they come with several benefits, which we will discuss later. Juicing, otherwise known as drinking smoothies, is for anyone. There are vegetarian and vegan recipes as well, that offer the energy and hydration that a person may be craving.

If you are serious about getting your life back, then the smoothies' recipes that are listed in this smoothie recipe book are going to be the starting point for your transformation. Through downloading this smoothie cookbook,you are going to start seeing a chance in your life...a change for the better.

BENEFITS OF DRINKING SMOOTHIES

There are several benefits to drinking smoothies as many people who have tried this diet are going to tell you. The good news is that smoothies can be changed in taste and ingredients to give you something that you cannot live without, so you do not have to worry about not liking what you are drinking. After all, the more you like the drink, the more likely you are going to be to continue to use the drink. With this being said, let's look at how smoothies are going to benefit you.

1. Smoothies when prepared properly are going to include ingredients that are going to ensure that you have boundless energy and vitality

2. Smoothies can help to improve the look of skin as it is getting the vitamins and nutrition needed to be look radiant

3. Your optimum health is going to be achieved as you are getting more of the nutrients that your body needs to function

4. Your ideal weight can be achieved with the use of smoothies

5. Along with weight loss, smoothies can help to gain muscle in the body

6. With smoothies you are meeting your daily intake of vitamins and minerals in a natural and safe method

The benefits of smoothies are going to continue to grow as more and more people are getting on board with this method of weight loss and overall health.

200 RECIPES

For those who are ready to start their journey with healthy smoothies, it is time to see what the entire smoothie world has to offer you.

Smoothies for Weight Loss

There are several smoothies for weight loss out there. Here are a few to get your started:

1. Delicious Mango

Ingredients:

¼ cup of mango cubes

¼ cup of mashed avocado

½ cup of mango juice

¼ cup of coconut yogurt

1 tbsp of lime juice, freshly squeezed

6 ice cubes

Instructions:

Put all the ingredients in a blender and blend until smooth, and then serve.

2. Simple Blueberry Smoothie

Ingredients:

1 cup of soymilk

1 cup of unsweetened blueberries, frozen are fine to use

1 tbsp of organic flaxseed oil

Instructions:

Combine soymilk and blueberries in blender, and then pour into glass. Add flaxseed oil and stir after other ingredients have been blended.

3. Peanut Butter Smoothie

Ingredients:

½ cup of soymilk

½ cup of coconut yogurt

2 tbsp of peanut butter, your favorite vegan brand

¼ of a super ripe banana

4 ice cubes

Instructions:

Blend until smooth and enjoy.

4. Blueberry and Yogurt Simple Smoothie

Ingredients:

1 cup of soymilk

6 ounces of coconut yogurt

1 cup of fresh blueberries

1 cup of frozen blueberries

1 tbsp of flaxseed oil

Instructions:

Blend the above ingredients until blended well and smooth. Then add in the 1 tablespoon of flaxseed oil for greater health benefits.

5. Decadent Chocolate and Raspberry Smoothie

Ingredients:

½ cup of soymilk

6 ounces of coconut yogurt

¼ cup of chocolate chips

1 cup of raspberries, fresh

1 cup of frozen raspberries

Instructions:

Blend ingredients together until smooth and then transfer to a cup. You may have to eat this more like ice cream due to the chocolate chips present in this recipe.

6. Smooth Peaches

Ingredients:

1 cup of soymilk

1 cup of frozen peaches, unsweetened

2 tsp of flaxseed oil

Instructions:

Blend the soymilk and peaches until smooth. Once transferred to a cup, add in the flaxseed oil and stir together, then serve.

7. Tangy and Sweet Smoothie

Ingredients:

1 cup of soymilk

6 ounces of coconut yogurt

Freshly squeezed lemon juice to taste

1 medium orange, sliced

Handful of ice

1 tbsp of flaxseed oil

Instructions:

Place all the ingredients into a blender, minus the flaxseed oil. Blend until smooth and transfer to glass. Stir in flaxseed oil for optimal weight loss results.

8. Simple Apple

Ingredients:

½ cup of soymilk

6 ounces of coconut yogurt

1 tsp of apple pie spice

1 medium apple, chopped

2 tbsp of cashew butter

Handful of ice

Instructions:

Chop apple, the combine all ingredients into the blender. Blend until smooth, and then serve.

9. Pineapple Delight

Ingredients:

1 cup of soymilk

4 ounces of pineapple tidbits

Handful of ice

1 tbsp of flaxseed oil

Instructions:

Combine soymilk, pineapple tidbits and ice into blender. After blending, pour into glass and add in the flaxseed oil. Serve immediately while cold.

10. Strawberry Sweet Smoothie

Ingredients:

1 cup of soy milk

1 cup of frozen strawberries

2 tsp of flaxseed oil

Instructions:

Blend together soymilk and strawberries. Once in a glass, pour in the flaxseed oil, stir and serve.

Smoothies that are Kid Friendly

Kids can enjoy the benefits of smoothies as well, and they can be used as a great source of vitamins and minerals for a child who is a picky eater. Here are some great recipes that kids are going to enjoy:

11. Strawberry Smoothies with Bananas

Ingredients:

½ bananas

½ cup of coconuts yogurt

1 cup of frozen strawberries

¼ cup of orange juice

Instructions:

Combine all the ingredients in a blender, and blend. Blend until frothy and serve immediately while cold.

12. Blazing Blueberry Smoothie

Ingredients:

½ cup of coconut yogurt

½ cup of soymilk

1 cup frozen blueberries

Instructions:

Combine all the ingredients in a blender. Blend this until frothy, then serve immediately.

13. Elvis Smoothie

Ingredients:

½ cup of coconut yogurt

½ cup of soymilk

½ bananas

1 tbsp of organic peanut butter

Handful of ice

Instructions:

Add ice, then pour other ingredients over the top of this and blend. Once blended smooth, serve immediately.

14. Citrus Smoothie

Ingredients

1 cubed mango or 1 cup of frozen mango cubes

¼ cup of orange juice

½ cup of coconut yogurt

Use ice if you are using a fresh mango, otherwise omit if frozen mango is used

Instructions:

Combine all the ingredients in a blender. Blend this until smooth and serve immediately.

15. Delightful Chocolate Smoothie

Ingredients:

8 ounces of almond milk, flavored vanilla

1 banana

2 tbsp of chocolate flavored peanut butter

Handful of ice

Instructions:

Put all the ingredients in the blender, blend this until smooth. Serve immediately for best taste.

16. Tropical Extravaganza Smoothie

Ingredients:

1½ cups of coconut milk

½ cup of frozen pineapple chunks

½ cup of ice cubes

3 medium fresh strawberries

1 tsp of lime juice

Instructions:

Place the entire ingredient in the blender. Use 'crush ice' setting to get this smooth. Then serve in a glass immediately.

17. Hidden Vegetables Smoothie

Ingredients:

½ cup of coconut yogurt

½ cup of soymilk

1 cup of kale or spinach leaves, chopped

1 cup of bananas, chopped

1 cup of frozen strawberries chopped

Instructions:

Place all the ingredients in a blender and blend until smooth. If the smoothie is too thick, add in a small amount of soymilk until you reach desired consistency. Then serve immediately.

18. Secret Fiber Smoothie

Ingredients:

2 or 3 ripe bananas, depending upon size, use your best judgment

4 ice cubes

2 tbsp of seeds, such as sunflower, flak, poppy or raw sesame seeds

Small amount of water to blend these smoothly together

Instructions:

Add in bananas, ice cubes and seeds to blend. Add a little water if this is too thick, and then serve when desired consistency has been achieved.

19. The Blue Smoothie

Ingredients:

1 cup of coconut yogurt

1 cup of fresh or frozen blueberries

½ cup of avocado

1 banana

½ cup of soymilk

½ tsp of cinnamon

4 to 6 ice cubes

Instructions

Mix all the ingredients in the blender and blend together well. Then serve, for an extra treat you can serve topped with whipped cream as a topper.

20. Peach Attack Smoothie

Ingredients:

3½ cups of chopped peaches, frozen

½ cup natural sweetener

1 tbsp of lemon juice

1 cup of coconut yogurt

Instructions:

Blend together. Once the desired consistency has been achieved, serve this immediately to maintain coolness.

21. Nutella and Strawberry Smoothie

Ingredients:

12 ounces of soymilk

2 tbsp of Nutella or other almond butter spread of your choice

4 strawberries

1 tsp of cocoa powder

½ cup of crushed ice

Instructions:

Blend together the Nutella and milk. Then add strawberries and ice to blend. Add in cocoa powder, and then pulse in blender. Serve immediately.

Skin Friendly Smoothies

Have you ever wanted a flawless complexion? If so, your skin is only as beautiful as what you eat. Here are several smoothies that can help with complexion and other types of skin issues:

22. Smoothie for Clear Skin

Ingredients:

1 scoop of hemp protein

½ cup of blueberries

½ bunch of dandelion greens without the stems

11 ounces of coconut water

¼ avocado

1 tbsp of cacao powder

Instructions:

Blend together until smooth. Then serve immediately to maintain coolness.

23. Anti-inflammatory Skin Smoothie

Ingredients:

1 tbsp of flaxseed oil

2 tbsp of raw almond butter

1 small banana

½ cup of apple juice

1 cup of ice cubes

Instructions:

Add in ice cubes, and then crush these in blender for best results. Add in the rest of the ingredients and blend until smooth.

24. Skin Boosting Smoothie

Ingredients:

1 tbsp of fish

½ cup of coconut yogurt

½ cup frozen mango cubes

½ cup of orange juice

½ cup of ice cubes

1 mint leaf

Instructions:

Add all ingredients together, including the mint leaf, shredding this leaf to ensure it mixes properly. Then blend, serve immediately. You can omit the mint leaf if you are not a fan of mint or have allergies.

25. Skin Antioxidants Smoothie

Ingredients:

1 tbsp of fish oil

½ cup of frozen strawberries

¼ cup of frozen blueberries

¼ cup of frozen raspberries

¼ cup of frozen bananas

¼ cup of chopped kale leaves

1 cup of water

Instructions:

Combine all the ingredients into the blender and blend. Serve immediately for best taste.

26. Tasty Skin Smoothie

Ingredients:

½ cup of hemp milk

½ cup of coconut milk or water

1 tbsp of hemp protein powder

1 pear, chopped

Handful of spinach or kale leaves

1 cup of ice

Instructions:

Ensure that the kale/spinach leaves are chopped, then add into blender along with the rest of the ingredients. Blend these until smooth and serve.

27. Vitamin C Infusion Smoothie

Ingredients:

1 cup of hemp milk

1 tbsp of hemp protein powder

1 orange that is peeled and sliced

½ avocado, peeled and sliced

Instructions:

Peel and slice orange and avocado, add all ingredients into the blender. Pulse or blend these together until desired consistency.

28. Probiotic Smoothie

Ingredients:

10 ounces of coconut water

Ice cubes, about a handful

4 ounces of frozen pineapple

1/8 tsp of ground cinnamon

1/8 tsp of nutmeg

Dash of vanilla stevia

Pinch of sea salt

Instructions:

Combine all ingredients together, and blend. Once it has reached desired consistency, drink immediately.

29. Anti-Aging Smoothie

Ingredients:

1 cup of yogurt

Lime juice to taste

1 cup of green tea that has cooled

½ cup of packed mint that is chopped

2 cups of ice cubes

Instructions:

Prepare green tea a head of time and allow to cool. Add in cooled green tea with remaining ingredients and blend. Serve immediately while cold.

30. Healthy Skin Smoothie

Ingredients:

1 chopped granny smith apple

1 banana

1 cup of orange juice

1 cup of coconut yogurt

½ cup of soymilk

1 tbsp of flaxseed oil

Instructions:

Cut and peel apple, then add into blender with remaining ingredients. Blend and serve immediately while cool.

31. Spicy and Sweet Smoothie

Ingredients:

3 green cardamom pods crushed

3 black peppercorns

3 cloves

1 allspice berry

½ tbsp. of grate ginger

1 cup of water

4 tbsp of maple syrup

16 ounces of kefir

Instructions:

Crush the cardamom pods, then add peppercorns, cloves, berry, ginger and water into a pot and simmer this. Let this cool, then add kefir and maple syrup into blender with the pot of ingredients and blend.

High in Fiber Smoothies

When wanting to improve your overall health, your digestive system must be on track. With these high fiber smoothies, you can help to reduce digestive troubles and become healthier.

32. Coffee Smoothie

Ingredients:

1 cup of your favorite coffee brew

1½ bananas, chunked

1 cup of coconut yogurt

1 tbsp of flaw seeds

½ tsp of cinnamon

¼ tsp of nutmeg

6 ice cubes

Instructions:

Blend your favorite coffee and let it cool. Then add all the ingredients into a blender. Blend until smooth and serve.

33. Digestive Power Smoothie

Ingredients:

1 ripe banana

1/3 cup of blueberries

1/3 cup of strawberries

½ cup of kale leaves

¼ cup of almond milk

1 tbsp of flax seeds

1 tbsp of hemp powder

1 tbsp of chia seeds

1 tbsp of acai

1 tsp of cinnamon

Instructions:

Add all ingredients into the blender and blend. If you want a more liquid type of smoothie, add in more water. Then serve.

34. The Green Monster

Ingredients:

1 small frozen banana

2 cups of baby spinach

1 tbsp of organic peanut butter

¾ cup of almond milk, vanilla flavored

½ cup of coconut yogurt

Instructions:

Blend together, you can add ice if you want this to be more thick. Once blended, serve while cool.

35. Hot Chocolate Smoothie

Ingredients:

12 ounces of coconut milk

1 mashed banana

1 scoop of protein powder

2 tbsp of cocoa powder

½ tsp of vanilla

Instructions:

Heat milk on stove until it starts to forma. While milk is heating, add the rest of the ingredients into a blender and blend. Gently pour the warm milk and puree together, until this is blended and smooth. Serve immediately.

36. Boost Smoothie

Ingredients:

6 ounces of coconut yogurt

8 almonds

½ cup of broccoli florets without the stems

1 cup of frozen strawberries

¼ cup of garbanzo beans

¾ cup of iced green tea

1 tsp of flax meal

¼ tsp of cinnamon

Instructions:

Pour all the ingredients into a blender, and then blend. You will want to serve this once it has reached your desired consistency and is still cold.

37. Berry Smoothie with Ginger

Ingredients:

1 cup of frozen cherries

1 cup of strawberries

1 cup of kale, chopped

1/8 cup of walnuts

1 tsp of wheat germ

½ tsp of grated ginger

¾ cup of green tea

Instructions:

Put everything into the blender and blend until smooth. Enjoy immediately for best taste.

38. A Mojito to Start Your Day off Right Smoothie

Ingredients:

½ cup of soymilk

1 frozen banana

1 cup of baby spinach

1 tsp of vanilla extract

½ lime, juiced

½ cup of spearmint

Ice cubes

Instructions:

Blend together the soymilk, banana, spinach, vanilla and lime juice. Once blended, add the spearmint and ice cubes. Then blend until smooth and serve.

39. Fig Smoothie

Ingredients:

½ cup of soymilk

½ cup of coconut yogurt

1 to 2 scoops of ice

4 fresh figs, with stems removed and halved

½ banana

1 date, pits removed

1 tsp of lemon juice

Dash of cinnamon

Instructions:

In the blender, put the soymilk, yogurt, ice, figs and banana, blend these for 30 seconds. Then add the date, lemon juice and cinnamon, blend until they are combined. Serve immediately.

40. Cinnamon Apple Smoothie

Ingredients:

8 ounces of coconut water

4 raw almonds

1 tsp vanilla

1 tsp cinnamon

1 cup of apple, chopped

½ scoop of protein powder

1 tbsp of flaxseed meal

Instructions:

Combine all the ingredients into the blender and blend well together. This is best if served the next morning, after being in the refrigerator all night.

41. Kiwi Explosion Smoothie

Ingredients:

3 ounces of yogurt of your choice

1 cup of baby spinach

½ cup frozen blueberries

½ cup of frozen mango

1 peeled kiwi

1/3 cup of kidney beans

1/8 cup of walnuts

1 tsp of flax meal

¾ cup of cold water

Instructions:

Pour everything together into a blender. Blend until smooth and your desired consistently have been met. Serve immediately.

Heart Happy Smoothies

The various ingredients in smoothies make them perfect for helping with certain health issues. This can be said of those who are looking to start eating and drinking more products that are heart healthy. Here are a few smoothies to get your heart on its way to being happier and healthier:

42. Green Happiness

Ingredients:

½ cup of water

2 tbsp. of flaxseeds

2 peeled clementine

1 banana

2 cups of spinach

½ cup of frozen pineapple chunks

Instructions:

Blend these together on medium low speed for around 10 seconds, then again on medium high speed from around 30 seconds. Serve once blended.

43. Up and Ready in the Morning Smoothie

Ingredients:

6 ounces of water

½ cup of vegan cottage cheese

1 tbsp chia seeds

1 tbsp of agave nectar

1 banana

1½ cups of cake that is chopped

1 cup of pineapple chunks

¾ cup of mango chunks

1 cup of ice cubes

Instructions:

Blend these together in the blender until they are at your desired consistency. Serve immediacy while cold.

44. Chocolate Treat for your Heart

Ingredients:

2/3 cup of coconut milk

¼ cup of agave nectar

1/3 cup of cocoa powder

4 dates, pitted

½ large avocado, peeled and pitted

3 cups of ice

Instructions:

Put the milk, nectar, powder, dates and avocado in the blender. Blend these on low. Then add in ice cubes and blend together to get the right consistency.

45. Orange Deliciousness

Ingredients:

1 cup of coconut milk

2 medium oranges, peeled

1 small yellow squash

1½ cup of ice cubes

6 ounces of frozen orange juice

Instructions:

Add all the ingredients into the blender, and blend for approximately for one minute until the desired consistency is reached.

46. Green Energy

Ingredients:

12 ounces of orange juice

1 apple

½ banana

1 cup of kale

1 cup of spinach

1 cup of frozen mango cubes

1 cup of ice cubes

Instructions:

Ensure all the kale and spinach is shredded, and then adds all ingredients into the blender. Blend this for around a minute, and then serve immediately while cold.

47. Red Velvet Smoothie

Ingredients:

2 cup of spinach

2 cups of coconut milk

2 cups of strawberry

4 dates, pitted

¼ cup of raw or cooked beets

1 tbsp of cacao powder

½ tsp of vanilla extract

Instructions:

First, blend together the spinach and coconut milk. Then add the remaining ingredients once the spinach and milk are smooth. Once blended, serve immediately.

48. It Takes Two to Mango Smoothie

Ingredients:

2 cups of fresh spinach

1½ cups of water

2 cups of frozen mango

1 orange, peeled

¼ cup of rolled oats

Instructions:

First blend together the spinach, orange and water. Once smooth, add in the remaining ingredients. Blend together and then serve once it reaches the desired consistency.

49. Beat the Blues Smoothie

Ingredients:

1 cup of coconut water

1 scoop of whey protein, your choice as to what you use

1 cup of frozen blueberries

¼ of an avocado

4 ice cubes

Instructions:

Place all ingredients in a blender, and then blend until smooth. Serve while this is still cold.

50. Peanut Butter Protein Smoothie

Ingredients:

½ cup of soymilk

2 tbsp of peanut butter, organic

2 tbsp of chocolate syrup

1 frozen banana

1 scoop of whey protein

8 ounces of coconut yogurt

Instructions:

Mix all ingredients in a blender, and blend until frothy. Serve immediately for best taste.

51. Carrot and Papaya Smoothie

Ingredients:

½ papaya

1 scoop of whey protein

¼ carrot juice

½ cup of berries, any type

4 ice cubes

Instructions:

Mix all the ingredients into the blender, and blend. Keep doing this until this is as smooth as you would like. Then serve.

Muscle Building Smoothies

For those who are trying to bulk up, who want to ensure their muscles are in tip-top shape, then these muscle building smoothies are just what you need to succeed.

52. Rise and Shine Smoothie

Ingredients:

1 cup frozen berries, an assortment can be used

1 orange, peeled

4 to 6 ounces of coconut yogurt

1 frozen banana

Instructions:

Put all ingredients in a blender, blend well, and then serve while cold.

53. Coconut Almond Smoothie

Ingredients:

1 cup of coconut milk

1 tbsp of coconut oil

½ frozen bananas

1 tbsp. of chia seeds

2 ice cubes

2 tbsp of almond butter

Instructions:

Place all the ingredients in the blender, and pulse until you get a frothy and smooth end. Serve while cold for best taste.

54. Protein Building Monster Smoothie

Ingredients:

1 frozen banana

1 cup of kale that has been chopped

1 tbsp of organic peanut butter

3/4 cup of vanilla almond milk

½ cup of coconut yogurt

2 cups of baby spinach, chopped

Instructions:

Chop vegetables as they should be, then place everything in the blender. Blend until frothy, and serve immediately.

55. Superfood Smoothie

Ingredients:

1½ cup of almond milk

1 handful of spinach leaves

1 tbsp of hemp

Ice as you need

1 cup of blueberries

Instructions:

Add in all ingredients minus the ice, then mix. Add in ice as you need to make this thicker for your tastes. Serve once you have reached the desired consistency.

56. PB&J Smoothie

Ingredients:

1 cup of frozen berries

1 scoop of vanilla whey protection

2 tbsp of rolled oats

1 cup of soy milk

1 tbsp of organic peanut butter

Instructions:

Mix all the ingredients together until they are smooth, then serve cold.

57. Pomegranate Protein Smoothie

Ingredients:

½ scoop of protein powder of your choice

1 cup water

3 tbsp of pomegranate seeds

3 tbsp of pomegranate juice

Handful of granola

1 cup of ice

Instructions:

Mix together all the ingredients within the blender, then serve while still cold for best taste.

58. Strawberry Dream Smoothie

Ingredients:

1 cup of frozen strawberries

½ cup of almonds, soaked overnight

½ cup of water

1 date

Instructions:

Soak the almonds in water overnight, and then peel these the next morning. Then add all ingredients to blender and blend. Serve immediately.

59. Sweet Protein and Carrot Smoothie

Ingredients:

½ cup of carrot juice

2/4 cups of almond milk

1 scoop of vanilla protein powder

Dash of cinnamon

4-5 cubes of ice

1 frozen banana

Instructions:

Add all ingredients to the blender and blend until smooth and frothy. Serve immediately while cold.

60. Sweet Treat Smoothie

Ingredients:

1 cup of almond milk

¼ cup of rolled oats

1 scoop of whey protein powder

Pinch of cinnamon

2 tbsp of cookie butter

3 tbsp of almond butter

8 ice cubes

Instructions:

Add all ingredients together in a blender and blend until smooth. Serve immediately.

61. Pick Me Up Smoothie

Ingredients:

½ cup of cashew milk

2/3 cups of ice cubes

½ tsp of vanilla

Dash of cinnamon

2 ounces of espresso

¼ cup of protein powder

½ frozen bananas

Instructions:

Blend together in a blender until smooth and frothy. Serve immediately while chilled for best taste.

Exercise Aiding Smoothies

After or before a workout, smoothies can be just what you need to ensure that your workout is a success and your body benefits from this workout. Here are a few to get you started:

62. Banana Bliss

Ingredients:

2 cups of soymilk

1 large banana

Handful of walnut pieces

Instructions:

Blend all the ingredients together and serve while cool.

63. The K Smoothie

Ingredients

1½ cups of soy milk

2 cups of kale, with stems and leaves

1 kiwi peeled

1 tbsp. of peanut butter, organic

1 tsp of agave nectar

Instructions:

Put all ingredients in a blender, and blend until smooth and frothy. Servia while chilled.

64. Cocoa Oat Smoothie

Ingredients:

¾ cup of soy milk

1 tsp of vanilla

½ cup of coconut yogurt

¼ cup of quick cook oats

1 tbsp of ground flaxseed

1 tsp of cocoa powder

Dash of cinnamon

1 small frozen banana

Instructions:

Start blending on low, then move onto high in order to get a smooth and frothy look.

65. Blast of Vitamin C Smoothie

Ingredients:

1 large grapefruit, cut into chunks and no seeds

½ crushed pineapple

½ strawberries, fresh or frozen

½ cup of plain yogurt

Instructions:

Place all ingredients in blender and blend until frothy and as smooth as you want. Then serve while chilled.

66. Energy Boosting Smoothie

Ingredients:

1 orange, chopped and peeled

1 lemon, chopped and peeled

4 spinach leaves

2 carrots, grated

1½ cup of almond milk

1 peach, peeled and chopped

Instructions:

Cut and peel fruits as stated, then place all ingredients in the blender. Blend these until smooth and serve immediately.

67. Spinach Strength Smoothie

Ingredients:

2 cups of frozen spinach broke into pieces

2 bananas

1 cup of apple juice

Instructions:

Blend all ingredients together, until frothy, and then serve.

68. All Red Smoothie

Ingredients:

4 beets that is cooked and peeled

2 cups of coconut water

2 cups of frozen strawberries

1 lime, juiced

Instructions:

Cook beets, and then juice lime. Add all ingredients into the blender and blend until smooth. Serve at once.

69. The Delicious Green

Ingredients:

½ cup of low fat coconut yogurt

2 cups of water

1 medium banana

1 cup of strawberries, slicked

2 cups of fresh spinach, chopped

Instructions:

Combine all the ingredients together and blend on high. Blend until spinach is chopped and the color is green. Serve immediately.

70. Blissful Sweet Smoothie

Ingredients:

1 banana

2 dried dates

2 cups of cold water

¼ cup of almonds

1 tbsp ground flaxseed

1 tbsp hemp protein

1 tbsp roasted carob powder

Instructions:

Add all ingredients into a blender and blend until frothy. Serve while chilled for best taste.

71. Olive Oil Smoothie

Ingredients:

1 cup of fresh spinach

1 small cucumber

¼ cup of parsley

1 stalk of celery

1 cup of water

Sea salt

3 to 4 tbsp of olive oil

Dash of cayenne pepper

Juice of ½ lemon

Instructions:

Place all ingredients in a blender and blend until smooth. This will not have a frothy appearance, more of a liquid. Drink this immediately.

Detox Smoothies

Detoxing is something that many people are trying to find more about, as it is meant to help you regulate your system and get back to normal. For those looking for detox smoothies, here are a few to start trying today.

72. Breakfast Smoothie for Winners

Ingredients:

1 cup of frozen raspberries

¾ cup of rice milk

¼ cup of cherries

2 tsp ground ginger

1 tsp of flaxseeds

1 to 2 tsp of fresh lemon juice

Instructions:

Add all ingredients into a blender and then blend until frothy and smooth. Serve in chilled glasses for refreshing taste.

73. The Original Green Detox Smoothie

Ingredients:

1¼ cup of chopped kale leaves

Lacinato

1¼ cups of cubed mango, frozen

2 medium ribs of celery, chopped

1 cup of fresh tangerine or orange juice

¼ cup of flat leaf parsley, chopped

¼ cup of chopped fresh mint

Instructions:

Combine all ingredients together in blender, puree until smooth, then pour into chilled glasses and drink immediately.

74. Green Giant Smoothie

Ingredients:

½ pear

¼ avocado

½ cucumber

½ lemon

Handful of cilantro

1 cup of kale

½ inch of ginger

½ cup of coconut water

1 scoop of protein water

Pure water

Instructions:

Blend together until frothy and foamy. Serve immediately or put into refrigerator to keep for a few days.

75. Sweet and Dark Smoothie

Ingredients:

½ banana

½ cup of blueberries

¼ avocado

½ cup of almond milk

1 tsp spirulina

1 scoop of protein powder

Pure water

Instructions:

Blend together until a dark color, then serve chilled.

76. Fiber Packed Smoothie

Ingredients:

½ pear

¼ avocado

1 cup of spinach

¼ cup of coconut water

1 cup of almond milk

1 tsp of chia seeds

1 scoop of protein powder

Pure water

Instructions:

Blend together until spinach is chopped and the entire drink is frothy. Serve chilled for best taste.

77. Probiotic Filled Smoothie

Ingredients:

1 cup papaya

1 cup coconut milk

½ lime juiced

Instructions:

Blend all ingredients and then serve chilled.

78. Vegetable Delight

Ingredients:

1 large cucumber

Fistful of kale

Fistful of romaine

2 stalks of celery

1 broccoli stem (large broccoli)

1 green apple

½ peeled lemon

Instructions:

Prepare the vegetables and two fruits that add taste. Then blend these together and serve cold.

79. Smooth Operator Smoothie

Ingredients:

1 avocado

1 banana

1 cup of blueberries

1 cucumber

Handful of kale, spinach or romaine lettuce

Coconut water

Sprinkle of cinnamon

Instructions:

Using a high speed, blend these ingredients together until smooth. Serve chilled.

80. Spicy and Nice Smoothie

Ingredients:

6 carrots

3 large tomatoes

2 red bell peppers

4 cloves garlic

4 stalks of celery

1 cup watercress

1 cup of spinach

1 red jalapeno (optional)

Instructions:

Wash and prepare vegetables. Then add all into the blender and blend until smooth and creamy.

81. Mint Apple Smoothie

Ingredients:

½ green apple

2 tbsp of hemp hearts

8 fresh mint leaves

3-4 leaves of lettuce

½ cup of a berry blend, your choice of what to use

8 to 12 ounces of water

Instructions:

Blend together well until frothy. Immediately serve while chilled.

Immunity Boosting Smoothies

There are several smoothies that you can utilize that are meant to help boost your immunity, which is important, especially during cold and flu season.

82. Orange Pineapple Dream

Ingredients:

1 cup of soy milk

½ cup of coconut yogurt

1 large orange, peeled and cubed

½ cup of frozen pineapple

Instructions:

Place all ingredients in blend and blend until smooth.

83. Green Tea Smoothie

Ingredients:

1 cup of frozen blueberries

1 cup of green tea, hot or cold

Instructions:

Prepare green tea if needed, then add all ingredients into blend. Blend until smooth and creamy. Then serve chilled.

84. Sunrise Smoothie

Ingredients:

1 cup of orange juice

1 cup of raspberries

½ cup of yogurt of your choice

1 cup of ice

Instructions:

Blend together, and then serve once smooth.

85. Refresh Your Immune System Smoothie

Ingredients:

3 cups of green tea

3 oranges with peels removed

½ cucumber

¼ cup of raw pumpkin seeds

2 handfuls of spinach

Instructions:

Place all ingredients into blender, then blend until smooth and serve.

86. Ruby Smoothie

Ingredients:

3 cups of green tea

1 large beet

2 apples

3 carrots

½ lemon with peel removed

2 hot peppers

Beet greens

Instructions:

Place all ingredients in blender and blend until smooth, serve chilled.

87. Boost Immunity Smoothie

Ingredients:

3 cups of green tea

1 banana

1 cup of blueberries

¼ cup of goji berries

1 broccoli stalk

2 tbsp of dulse

3 handfuls of spinach

Instructions:

Combined ingredients in blender and blend. Serve chilled.

88. Orange Goji Berry Smoothie

Ingredients:

2 cups of water

2 oranges, with the peels removed

Handful of goji berries

2 handfuls of spinach

Instructions:

Blend tougher in blender and serve while cold.

89. Power Up with Berry and Coconut Smoothie

Ingredients:

Handful of frozen blueberries

Half a banana

3 ice cubes

¾ cup of coconut water

2 tbsp of coconut milk

1 tbsp of chia seeds

Dash of cinnamon

Instructions:

Blend tougher for two minutes until smooth, then serve.

90. Cleanse Out Smoothie

Ingredients:

1 orange peeled

1 green apple with the skin on

2 handfuls of baby spinach

½ lemon, peeled

Pinch of ginger

3 ice cubes

Pinch of parsley

Instructions:

Blend for one minute and then serve while chilled.

91. Go Wild Smoothie

Ingredients:

2 cloves of garlic

¼ inch of ginger

Handful of parsley

4 carrots

1 apple

Instructions:

Mix together for a few minutes in blender until smooth, then serve chilled.

Fruit Only Smoothies

For those who love fruit, then these smoothies are going to be their absolute favorites!

92. Crazy for Bananas

Ingredients:

½ cup of yogurt of your choice

2 bananas

A pinch of cinnamon

1 cup of ice

Instructions:

Blend together and smooth immediately once smooth.

93. Duo Smoothie

Ingredients:

1 banana

1 cup of frozen or fresh strawberries

½ cup of soy milk

½ cup of yogurt

1 cup of ice

Instructions:

Blend together until smooth and serve immediately.

94. Banana Surprise

Ingredients:

1 cup of frozen banana

1 cup of frozen peach

1 cup of frozen mango

1 cup of yogurt

1 cup of ice

Instructions:

Blend together and then serve once desired consistency has been met.

95. Mango Delight

Ingredients:

2 mangos, fresh or frozen cubed

1 cup of almond milk or coconut water

1 cup of ice

Instructions:

Mix together until smooth and enjoy.

96. Pretty in Pink Smoothie

Ingredients:

1 cup of almond milk

½ cup of orange juice

1½ cup of frozen raspberries

Instructions:

Add into blender and blend until smooth, then serve while chilled.

97. Peanut Butter Blueberry Smoothie

Ingredients:

2 tbsp of whey protein

1 banana

½ cup of blueberries

1 tbsp of peanut butter

¼ cup of almond milk

1 cup of ice

Instructions:

Blend together well and serve once smooth.

98. Banana Mango Smoothie

Ingredients:

1 cup of frozen mango

½ banana

¼ cup of almond milk

1 cup of ice

Instructions:

Combine the ingredients into a blender, blend until smooth.

99. Watermelon Strawberry Smoothie

Ingredients:

1 cup of cubed watermelon

1 cup of frozen strawberries

¼ cup of almond milk

Instructions:

Add ingredients into a blender, then blend until smooth and enjoy!

100. Sparkling Watermelon Smoothie

Ingredients:

2 cups of cubed watermelon

1 cup of yogurt

2 tbsp of shredded coconut

2 cups of sparkling water

1 cup of ice

3 leaves of fresh mint

Instructions:

Blend until the ingredients are smooth and serve chilled.

101. Stay Peachy Smoothie

Ingredients:

1 cup of frozen peaches

½ cup of coconut yogurt

Juice of 1 lime

Splash of vanilla extract

Instructions:

Add together and blend until smooth, serve chilled.

Veggie Smoothies

If you love your vegetables, or even if you are not a big fan, you will find something that is worth drinking with these veggie smoothies.

102. Cucumber Spa Smoothie

Ingredients:

2 medium cucumbers, chopped, seeded and peeled

Juice of 1 lime

½ cup water

1 cup of ice

Instructions:

Prepare the cucumbers, and then place all ingredients in blender and blend until smooth. Serve while chilled.

103. Super Green Smoothie

Ingredients:

Handful of kale

Handful of spinach

¼ cup of almond milk

2 tsp of chia seeds

1 cup of ice

Instructions:

Blend together until smooth and creamy. Then serve chilled.

104. Yam Smoothie

Ingredients:

1 cup of yams, cooked or canned

1 cup of ice

Dash of cinnamon for taste

Instructions:

Simply combine all ingredients and blend until smooth, then enjoy.

105. Zucchini Simplicity Smoothie

Ingredients:

1 zucchini, steamed without peel

¼ cup of almond milk

1 cup of ice

2 cubes of orange for taste

Instructions:

Blend all the ingredients together and then serve chilled.

106. Broccoli Smoothie

Ingredients:

1 cup of broccoli florets

½ cucumber, peeled and cubed

Handful of grapes for sweetness

1 lime, juiced

Instructions:

Place all ingredients in blender and blend until smooth, then enjoy.

107. Salad Smoothie

Ingredients:

1 cup of water

½ orange, peeled to add some sweetness

1 cup of spinach, fresh

½ beet

1/3 cup of baby carrots

1/3 cup of cauliflower florets

1/3 cup of broccoli florets

1 stalk celery

½ lime, peeled

1 tbsp of chia seeds

Instructions:

Blend tougher for about one minute to make smooth, then serve chilled.

108. Rhubarb Smoothie

Ingredients:

1 cup of frozen rhubarb

1 small banana

1 cup of cranberry juice

½ cup of yogurt, of your choice

Instructions:

Blend all ingredients together until smooth and enjoy!

109. Veggie Delicious Smoothie

Ingredients:

1 cup of water

1 tomato, chopped

1 large carrot

1 cup of kale

2 radishes

1 lemon, peeled

6 ice cubes

Instructions:

Mix together well and then serve once smooth and blended.

110. Cabbage Smoothie

Ingredients:

1 cup of chopped cabbage

1 cup of red grapes

1 red apple

1 large carrot

½ cup water

½ cup of ice

1 tbsp of fresh ginger

Instructions:

Add into blender and blend until smooth, then serve.

111. Zucchini and Carrot Delight Smoothie

Ingredients:

1 zucchini, peeled and chopped

1 carrot, peeled and chopped

½ cup of plain Greek yogurt

½ cup of soy milk

2 tbsp of rolled oats

1 tbsp of flax seeds

Instructions:

Add all ingredients into blender and blend well until smooth.

112. Spinach Smoothie with a Fruit Blast

Ingredients:

2 cups of frozen spinach leaves

2 bananas, cut into chunks

1 ounce of tofu

2 tbsp of coconut

½ cup of frozen peaches

½ cup of frozen pineapple

½ cup of frozen mango

½ cup of frozen strawberries

1 cup of apple juice to taste

Instructions:

Add all ingredients into blender and then blend until smooth. Serve chilled.

Simple Smoothies

If you do not have the time to blend together something that is magnificent, do not fear as some of the best smoothies out there are simple to make.

113. Triple Berry Surprise

Ingredients:

1½ cups of mixed berries, such as strawberries, blackberries, raspberries

1 cup of soy milk

Instructions:

Mix together, blend and serve immediately.

114. Almond Smoothie

Ingredients:

1 cup of almond milk

1 cup of ice

Instructions:

Mix together and blend. Serve chilled once desired consistency has been reached.

115. Cantaloupe Smoothie

Ingredients:

2 cups of cubed cantaloupe

½ lime, juiced

2 tbsp of sweetener

1 cup of ice

½ cup of water

Instructions:

Mix together in blender, then blend until smooth and serve chilled.

116. The Apple Carrot Smoothie

Ingredients:

1 cup of carrot juice

1 cup of apple juice

1½ cup of ice

Instructions:

Combine all ingredients into the blender and blend until smooth.

117. Creamy Date Smoothie

Ingredients:

¾ of soy milk

1/3 cup of pitted dates

½ cup of ice

Instructions:

Add together into blender and blend until smooth.

118. Simply Mango Smoothie

Instructions:

1 cup of ripe mango

½ cup of soy milk

½ cup of ice

¼ cup of yogurt of your choice

Instructions:

Place together in blender and blend until smooth and frothy.

119. Apple Kale Smoothie

Ingredients:

¾ cup of chopped kale

1 small stalk of celery

½ banana

½ cup of apple juice

½ cup of ice

Instructions:

Place into blender and blend until smooth. Then serve chilled.

120. Banana Cashew Smoothie

Ingredients:

¼ cup of raw cashews, no salt

1 cup of ice

½ banana

1 tbsp of maple syrup

Instructions:

Add together in blender and blend until smooth.

121. Nutty Raspberry Smoothie

Ingredients:

¾ cup of soy milk

¾ cup of frozen raspberries

½ banana

1 tbsp of almond butter

Instructions:

Add all ingredients into blender and blend until smooth. Serve immediately.

122. Flax Strawberry Smoothie

Ingredients:

1 cup of frozen strawberries

¾ cup of yogurt

½ cup of orange juice

1 tbsp of flax seed

Instructions:

Add all ingredients together and blend until smooth. Serve immediately while chilled.

CONCLUSION

Thank you again for downloading this book! I hope this book was able to help you to start making smoothies that help to balance your life and make you healthier. Whether you are simply looking to lose weight or want to drink smoothies as way to get your health conditions under control, there are tons of smoothies that are going to fit your needs.

The next step is to fill up your grocery cart with tasty fruits and vegetables. Then start to enjoy these delicious smoothies that are going to benefit your health.

If you have enjoyed this book, I ask that you leave a review so that others can benefit from the wealth of knowledge within this ebook as well.

www.ingramcontent.com/pod-product-compliance
Lightning Source LLC
Chambersburg PA
CBHW071441070526
44578CB00001B/176